Daisy Hooee Nampeyo

By Carol Fowler

DILLON PRESS, INC.
MINNEAPOLIS, MINNESOTA

[redacted]

Second printing 1978

Dillon Press, Inc., 500 South Third Street
Minneapolis, Minnesota 55415

Printed in the United States of America

Library of Congress Cataloging in Publication Data

Fowler, Carol.
Daisy Hooee Nampeyo.

(The Story of an American Indian)
SUMMARY: A biography of the Hopi Indian artist famous for her pottery, sculpture, and jewelry.
1. Nampeyo, Daisy Hooee, 1910- —Juvenile literature. 2. Hopi Indians—Biography—Juvenile literature. 3. Artists—Arizona—Biography—Juvenile literature. [1. Nampeyo, Daisy Hooee, 1910- 2. Hopi Indians—Biography. 3. Indians of North America—Biography. 4. Artists] I. Title.
E99.H7F64 730'.092'4 [B] [92] 76-54809
ISBN 0-87518-141-4

ON THE COVER:

Daisy Hooee Nampeyo decorating a Hopi pot in the traditional way with a yucca fiber brush and paint made from dried bee weed.

DAISY HOOEE NAMPEYO

A noted potter, Daisy Hooee Nampeyo is passing on her art to her children and grandchildren, as she and her sisters in turn had learned it from their grandmother, Nampeyo.

Threatened with blindness when she was twelve years old, she left the Hopi reservation in northern Arizona to have corrective surgery performed in California. Her friendship with a wealthy patron of the arts led to studies abroad in painting and sculpture.

When she returned to Arizona as a young woman, she took up pottery making, a craft she had learned as a child. Moving to Zuni, New Mexico, in the late 1930s, she brought her skill as a sculptor to carving turquoise, coral, and jet. Some years later she began making pottery again in both the Hopi and Zuni styles.

Daisy Hooee Nampeyo is nationally recognized as an innovative and brilliant potter, working within the ancient traditions of the Pueblo Indians. She teaches pottery making to the women of Zuni and travels widely to give demonstrations in art schools and museums.

Contents

CHAPTER I

People Of The Short Blue Corn

Fierce winds howl and shriek over the high desert mesas of the Hopi Reservation in northern Arizona. Day after day they swirl from the northwest and carry sand that stings one's cheeks and eyes. Sometimes the winds gather so much force that it is frightening to walk along the narrow rocky spine of First Mesa from the village of Hano to Walpi, at the tip of the mesa.

But First Mesa is a place of great beauty as well as harshness. On many days the sun shines brilliantly, and from the flat roofs of the stone and adobe houses one can see the distant San Francisco peaks, sacred home of the masked Hopi gods. Just below the mesa clumps of corn and squash grow in the dry soil. Beyond the fields cottonwoods mark the thin line of Polacca Wash. They shimmer silver-green in the summer and gold in the autumn. And beyond everything the gently rolling desert stretches endlessly like a giant blanket to the edge of the world.

Nampeyo, the Hopis' most famous potter, captured the beauty, the strength, and the colors of this Hopi world in her pottery. The pots were golden tan like the stone villages, and their red and brown designs recalled colors of the desert floor. Nampeyo painted bold designs, as bold and clear as the outlines of the mesas and buttes. She used clay from the mesa and paints from desert plants, so that her pottery was part of the desert itself. Molded and formed by Nampeyo's hands, the clay became something useful and something beautiful.

During the early 1900s Nampeyo lived and worked in Hano. On warm summer days the people of the village would see her sitting on a blanket in front of her house making pottery with her little granddaughter Daisy. As they worked, Nampeyo told Daisy stories about the Hopis. Young Daisy learned to make pottery, and she learned about the Hopi people from Nampeyo.

One of the stories told by the Hopis—and a very ancient one—foretold the difficult history of the Hopis as they scratched a living from the dry desert soil. When the

View from First Mesa.

Indian peoples first climbed into their present dwelling place from the world beneath this world, each tribe chose an ear of corn.

The Navajos picked the long yellow ear with full, juicy kernels, which symbolized a prosperous, but short life. The Comanches took the red corn, and the Utes chose flint corn. The Hopis, the last to choose, found only a short, stubby ear of blue corn left. They knew that although it meant a hard life, it also meant a long life.

In many ways the prophecy in the legend has proven to be true. The Hopis have lived a life of hardship in one of the most dry, barren parts of the high desert plateau of the Southwest. No streams water their fields. They depend entirely on the few inches of rain that fall in violent thundershowers during the summer. Springs supply their drinking water. But indeed, as a tribe, they have had a long life. Oraibi, one of the Hopi villages, is possibly the oldest continuously inhabited settlement in the United States. Only Acoma, an Indian village in New Mexico, is able to make the same claim. Both villages were settled around A.D. 1100.

Exactly when the Hopis built the villages where they now live, or how they became a distinct group of people with their own language, religion, and culture, is clouded in time and memory. Yet scientists are able to reconstruct a Hopi history. By examining what has been left behind by ancestors of the Hopis, they learn many things about the everyday life of these people. Tumbled stones and timbers tell about the size and shape of their houses. Tree rings of log beams are compared to a master chart to give their age. Seeds and bones give clues to the diet of the early Hopis. Designs on the broken pottery fragments, called potsherds, even show what was beautiful to these ancient people.

Hopi legends are another source of useful information. Generally rooted in some event that actually happened, these stories do not describe accurate details of what happened long ago. Instead, they tell why things happened. They tell what made people act as they did. And they teach a lesson. If the people made the right choice, they were rewarded. But if they acted contrary to the Hopi Way, they were punished. Since the Hopis did not have a written language, they never wrote the stories down. But they told them over and over again, from parent to child. Hopis living in modern times have also told the stories to anthropologists, those scientists who study different human cultures. Using all of these sources of information, the anthropologists then piece the fragments together, until like a puzzle, the picture of the Hopi past emerges.

Anthropologists generally believe that the ancestors of American Indians migrated from Asia to the North American continent across the Bering Strait thousands of years ago. These ancient people migrated southward very slowly, sometimes settling for long periods in one spot. The ancestors of the Hopis probably traveled along the west coast of what is now the United States and then worked their way inland. By about the fourth century A.D., they had settled the San Juan River Valley, which cuts east to west through the red rock canyons of southern Utah. The name Basketmaker is given to these people since they gathered their food—wild seeds and berries—in baskets woven out of reeds, stems, and roots. They made hunting spears and arrows out of bone or chipped them out of rock.

The Basketmakers lived in caves, usually large open

An Anasazi village. Note the overhanging cliff and the round, sunken kiva.

hollows eroded out of the sides of cliffs. When their enemies threatened, the Basketmakers climbed to safety up ladders that led to their cave openings. Then they pulled the ladder behind them, cutting off the entrance to their shelters. Gradually they began to pile up stones to close off the front of the caves, so that the cliff shelter became an enclosed room. Later they joined these rooms with other caves until they had an entire "apartment house," clinging to the side of the cliff.

Anasazi pottery.

By the twelfth century the Hopi ancestors lived in large stone and adobe settlements. They had taken up farming, and they grew corn, beans, and squash for food and cotton for clothing. They made thin-walled, durable pottery, decorated in abstract designs. The people had also developed a religious system. Ceremonies and rituals took place in kivas—round, underground chambers that were entered by a ladder through an opening in the roof. The shape of the chamber reminded the people of the underground world where they had previously lived. A damp spot in the center of the floor symbolized the place where they had emerged into the present world. Groups of people called clans observed ceremonies together.

According to Hopi legend, the clans formed during earlier migrations. When one tiny band of people came upon the carcass of a bear, they saw it as a sign that they should become the Bear Clan, which is still one of the leading Hopi Clans. There are many clans named for animals and plants and others with names relating to water, so important to the growth of crops. All of the clans have their own legends and ceremonies. Most of the rituals are aimed at pleasing the spirits so they will allow the rain to fall. Like most American Indians, Hopis believe that spirits live in everything—plants, animals, earth, and sky. Pleasing the spirits and living in harmony with them are the aims of the Hopi religion.

The people who lived in the San Juan Valley became known as the Anasazi, and they were the ancestors not only of the Hopis but also of several other Indian groups in the American Southwest. Even after they built their large settlements, the Anasazi were restless. They abandoned their stone settlements for reasons that remain a mystery and built others just as large and complex. Groups of people left the valley from time to time and settled elsewhere. Other groups joined them. In the thirteenth century, a long drought apparently caused the people still living in the San Juan Valley to desert their villages, and the Anasazi culture came to an end.

During the long period of resettlement, those people who became the Hopi migrated slowly to the Black Mesa in northern Arizona. Those who traveled to western New Mexico became the Zuni. Still others settled farther east in the Rio Grande River Valley. Gradually, over the centuries, their languages and customs changed. By the time the Spanish came to the region in the early sixteenth century, they had formed as many as eighty independent settlements. All of these different groups are now known as the Pueblos, a Spanish word meaning village. They are all governed separately, and they have their own clan systems and religious ceremonies. But because they share common ancestors, there are similarities in their customs.

Black Mesa, the homeland of the Hopi, is a high, flat tableland that juts out of a rolling plain. The Bear Clan arrived there first and built Oraibi on top of Third Mesa, one of the three cliffs that reach out like fingers southward over the desert. The stone and adobe houses were like those of the San Juan Valley. Each house had several rooms; the openings were in the roof. Ladders leaned against the side of the houses so that people could climb up to the openings. When enemies threatened, the Hopis pulled up the ladders and escaped into their houses, just as they had once escaped into their cave dwellings.

In time other clans arrived and asked for permission to stay at Oraibi. If their ceremonies were helpful to the people of Oraibi, the Bear Clan chief gave them permission to stay. If not, they moved on, sometimes building villages on the other cliffs of Black Mesa. In time Hopi villages stretched from Oraibi to Awatovi, twenty-five miles to the east.

One of these villages, Sikyatki, sprawled in a narrow valley beside First Mesa. The village prospered. Rain fell on its corn, squash, and bean fields, and fine pottery was made. Sikyatki women were so expert at making pottery that the smoke from pottery fires rose over the village nearly every day. Using the creamy yellow clay found nearby, the women shaped large round jars, decorating them in brown and red designs. And then suddenly, for some unknown reason, Sikyatki was abandoned. Today when scientists study its ruins, they find no charred timbers that indicate a fire. The tumbled stones appear to be an effect of time and not caused by violent attack. The ghost village offers no clues to the people's sudden flight.

Hopi legends, however, describe the flight from Sikyatki. More than one version of the story is still told in the Hopi villages. While the details of the legends vary, their lesson is the same. Because of murder and violence, things did not go well in Sikyatki. Stones from the mesa tumbled into the spring. The rain stopped, and the fields dried up. The clans left Sikyatki, their beautiful pottery, and the evil committed there.

Some of the clans migrated to the south and then west. Eventually the Coyote Clan came to Oraibi and settled there. Others traveled to the Rio Grande Valley; some simply disappeared. Within walking distance of all of the present Hopi villages, there are settlements like Sikyatki that were abandoned. No one knows exactly why the people left, but in each case the Hopi stories tell of evil coming among the people so that they no longer followed the Hopi Way, the peaceful way. Their ignorance of the actual events does not concern the Hopis. To them, the truth is found in the evil that upset the Hopi Way.

For many years the Hopi people lived at the edge of the three fingers of Black Mesa, tilling their crops in the fields below and climbing the mesas to the villages at night. Religious ceremonies claimed most of the time and attention not given to farming. They still made pottery, but it was not as beautiful as Sikyatki pottery had been. Then one day, armed white men riding horses appeared from the southeast. The Hopis advanced to meet them, sprinkling sacred cornmeal in the path of the horses. They expected the white men to stop at the cornmeal for a welcoming ceremony. But the white men, the Spaniards, or Castillas, as the Hopis called them, did not understand and charged the Hopis. In 1598 a man who represented the Spanish government "received the submission" of the Hopi villages for the King of Spain. This means that the Hopis accepted Spain's claim to the land, or at least, the Spaniards saw it that way.

The soldiers left after a time, but a few years later the Spanish missionaries came and stayed. The Spanish priests forced the Hopis to build the mission. The Hopis had to drag heavy juniper logs, used for roof beams, from mountains forty miles away. The logs left deep marks in the sandstone mesa that can be seen to this day. The Hopis called the building the slave church, because they felt they were slaves in being forced to do all the labor.

After the church was completed, the missionaries baptized the Hopi people and demanded that they attend mass. They beat those who stayed away. When the Hopis held their ceremonies in the kivas, the priests elbowed their way inside and told them that the ceremonies were evil. The missionaries thought they were doing the right thing in forcing the Hopis to become Christians, but the Hopis believed it was their duty to observe the cycle of rituals and ceremonies that they had practiced for centuries. If they neglected the dances or the offering of prayer sticks to the spirits, the rain would not fall. The crops would not grow, and the springs would dry up. Without the ceremonies the young people would forget the Hopi Way.

Finally many chiefs of the Pueblo villages met. They decided something had to be done to restore their former way of life. Chiefs from the Rio Grande and Hopi villages were given a long rope with many knots. As the Hopis returned to Black Mesa from the Rio Grande Valley, they untied one knot a day. In this way, the widely separated villages could plan their revolt against Spanish rule for the same day.

On the day the last knot was unraveled, Hopi warriors attacked the three missions that had been established in their villages of Oraibi, Shongopovi, and Awatovi. They killed the priests, tore down the buildings, and buried the altar vessels. The clans divided the horses and sheep, peach trees and grape vines, and metal tools and weapons that the Spaniards left behind. The coordinated Indian attack successfully drove the Spaniards back to Mexico in what became known as the Pueblo Rebellion of 1680.

Their freedom was short-lived. In 1692 the Spaniards again marched northward and reconquered most of the Pueblo villages. According to tradition, Oraibi never bowed again to the Spaniards. When the missionaries returned they built a church only at Awatovi. Again, they divided families, split clans, and broke up the Hopi religious ceremonies. Once more, they were driven out in an attack so violent that Awatovi was burned and destroyed. To this day the Hopis do not like to talk about the destruction of Awatovi. By nature they are a peaceful people. They resorted to warlike behavior only when they believed their Hopi Way to be seriously threatened.

Soon after the Spaniards reconquered the Pueblo peoples, a band of Tewa-speaking people from the Rio Grande Valley migrated to First Mesa. At first the Hopi village of Walpi did not welcome the Tewas, and the village chief would not let them settle on top of the mesa. But he changed his mind after the Tewas drove away a band of Utes who attacked Walpi in hopes of getting corn and sheep.

The Tewas built their village, called Hano, a short distance from Walpi. Because their reception on First Mesa had been cool, the Tewa people decided to stay to themselves. They especially wanted to keep their religious ceremonies secret from the Hopis. The men of Hano gathered and dug a deep pit. Then each man lined up and, one by one, they spit into the hole. The dirt was shoveled back into the pit, stamped down, and the men of Hano took a large rock and pounded the dirt over the pit as hard as they could. They said that they had buried their language with their spit. The Hopis would never be able to speak Tewa, although the people of Hano would speak both languages.

To this day, even if a man of Walpi marries a Hano woman and lives in her household, he is unable to learn the Tewa language, although his wife and his children speak it. Proud of their heritage, the Tewa-Hopi repeat this legend each year at their winter solstice ceremony, which takes place on the shortest day of the year in December.

Other than keeping their religious ceremonies separate, the people of Hano and Walpi got along peacefully. Living many desert miles away from the Rio Grande Valley, where most of the Spaniards had settled, the Hopis were little affected when Mexico won its independence from Spain in 1821. Then in 1846, during the Mexican War, the Americans gained the area that stretched from Texas to California, including Black Mesa.

In 1882 the United States government formed the Hopi Indian Reservation, and five years later founded a boarding school for Indian children nearby. Most Hopis ignored the school. Sometimes soldiers came to try to force the Hopi children to attend school. This angered the Hopis as much as the missionaries had.

By the turn of the century, some of the Hopis, especially the Tewa-Hopis of Hano, thought it was to their benefit to learn English and to learn the Americans' way of doing things. They encouraged their children to attend school, and they often sought out contact with white people. Modern livestock raising techniques and working for wages increased their prosperity. Some of the Tewa-Hopi who had learned to speak English served as interpreters for the entire tribe. Modern communities with cement block houses and running water sprung up at the base of the mesas, but most of the Hopis kept an old family house in the villages on the mesa top. In a cycle that repeats year after year, they return to perform the rituals and ceremonies in the kivas and the religious dances in the villages, just as their ancestors did before white people set foot in North America.

CHAPTER II

Life On Top

In 1910 the people of Hano still lived in the old way on top of First Mesa. When Daisy was born, she and her mother stayed in a darkened room for twenty days. The Hopis believed that like bean seedlings, which take ten days to emerge from the soil and then must be shaded from the bright sun for ten more days, human infants need to be shielded from the light in order to grow. Her father's sisters took care of her and gave the baby her Hopi name. They chose Tobacco Flower because her father belonged to the Tobacco Clan.

Until the United States took over Hopi lands and formed the reservation, Hopis had only one name, which was given to them by their father's female relatives. Daisy's grandparents, Nampeyo and Lesou, had only one name during their lifetimes. But the white people who worked at the government agency and schools required the Hopis to have two names—a first name and a family name. Daisy's father took the name Willie Healing, and his wife was known as Annie Healing. Daisy received her American name from the field nurse at the government agency on First Mesa. When she was old enough to go to school, she would be Daisy Healing, but until then, her name was Tobacco Flower.

Although Daisy was named after her father's clan, she belonged to the clan of her mother. All of Annie Healing's six children became lifetime members of the Corn Clan at birth. Clan membership and property were handed down through the female side of the family. The fields where Willie Healing planted squash, corn, melons, and beans were owned by Nampeyo and located in the area set aside for the Corn Clan. The oldest woman of each family chose the fields she wanted and then divided the fields between her daughters and their families.

Willie Healing had to be a clever farmer to raise enough to feed his family. Farming on the high desert around First Mesa was difficult. The fields had to be located where water seeped down from the mesa, or where there might be just enough flooding during rain storms to water the corn without washing it away. Hopi corn is planted in clumps rather than rows and appears short and stunted in the sandy soil. Because there is so little water, the clumps are set far apart. Often they need to be protected from the fierce winds by a line of brush.

Besides farming in the short growing season, Willie raised cattle, which were kept on distant Hopi ranch lands. When the cattle needed to be herded or dehorned, both Willie and Annie went to the ranch. Daisy's mother owned the land, but her father owned the cattle and wagons that belonged to the family.

Like other Hopi babies, Daisy swung on a cradle board during the early months of her life. Hung from the vigas, the round logs that form the base of the roof, the cradle board was nudged by anyone who passed it. The gentle motion and the activity of the family kept Hopi babies

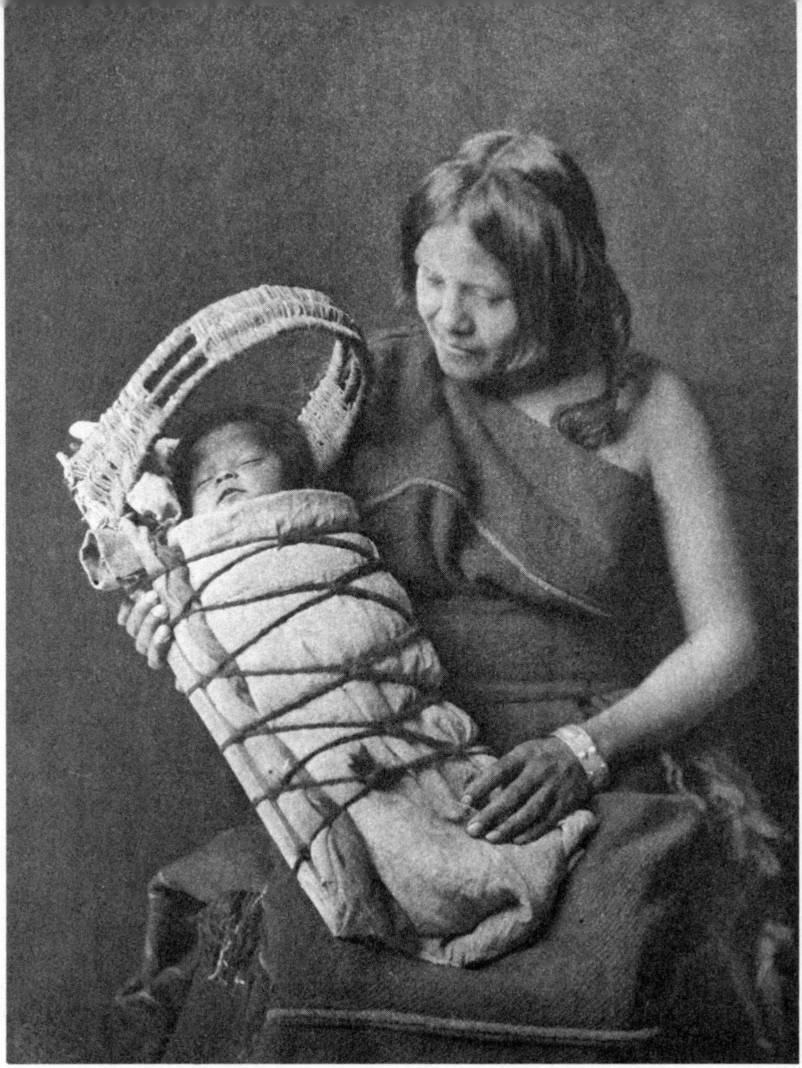

A Hopi baby in a cradle board.

happy. If Annie needed to go out, she wrapped Daisy in a shawl and carried her on her back. When she learned to walk, Daisy's bare feet touched the hand-patted adobe floor of the house. The rooms stayed cool in the summer because the thick rock walls insulated them against the heat of the desert sun. During the winter the walls held the heat from fires in the stove.

The inside walls of the house were plastered with adobe

mud and whitewashed. Annie Healing took pride in keeping the walls as white as possible. Each spring she dug calcimine out of the side of the mesa, then sifted it, mixed the white powder with water, and painted the walls. The fresh smell of newly painted whitewash is one of Daisy's earliest memories.

The whitewashed walls were nearly bare except for some household items that hung within easy reach and a few brightly painted kachina dolls. The dolls were given to the children of the family so that they would recognize kachinas, the masked figures that represented spirits in the Hopi dances.

When Daisy first saw the kachinas at a nighttime dance, she thought they were real.

A Hopi kachina doll.

The snake kachinas danced and played tricks to show how strong they were, and mudheads, a kind of clown, danced with them. The snake kachinas threw the mudheads down and bit them. When the mudheads got up, they were thrown down again. It was exciting but it was very frightening, too.

Another time her grandmother took her along the path that led from Hano to Walpi to see a velvet shirt dance. The wind blew over the mesa, and sand stung their faces. Daisy hid her face deep in her blanket. When they got to Walpi, she thought the dance was very beautiful. But she was so uncomfortable in the cold wind that she wrapped up in her blanket and started to walk home. Nampeyo called to her. She warned Daisy that she might take the wrong path and get lost, or she could be blown off the path at the narrow place in the mesa. Daisy hurried back to the safety of her grandmother's lap.

These dances and ceremonies that Daisy watched served as calendars for the Hopi people. Time was measured by planting and harvesting and the dances and prayers for enough rain to insure good crops. During midsummer when the corn was growing, the last kachina dance, the Niman, took place in the village. If the dance was done properly and the kachinas pleased the spirits, then the spirits would allow rain to fall. After Niman, the Hopis believed that the spirits of the kachinas returned to their homes in the San Francisco mountains. No more masked dances were held until the kachina season started all over again the following winter.

Other rain dances, including the famous Hopi Snake Dance, continued during the growing and harvest seasons,

Daisy's grandfather, Lesou, starting down the steep trail for water at Hano, the village where Daisy was born.

but the dancers did not wear masks. When the days grew very short and the sun dipped to its lowest point in the southern sky, the Soyal ceremony was held. During this ceremony, which took several days in December, the priests offered prayers and chants to coax the sun back.

When Daisy toddled along the streets of Hano to visit Nampeyo, she passed by houses built of tan stone dug from the mesa top. The houses looked as if they were a part of the mesa itself. Bright strings of red peppers and many-colored ears of dried corn hung on the stone walls. The flat roofs made fine places to sit and watch the dances or just the coming and going of people in the village. The top of the kiva wall was a favorite place for Nampeyo to sit. Sometimes Daisy would see her sitting there and hear her calling to her. Then Daisy teased her grandmother by running up very close to the kiva wall while Nampeyo continued to call in a loud voice.

Daisy's memories of her early years are about these things—the old house on top—her name for the house in Hano—her family, and the dances in the village.

During her childhood the Healing family moved to Polacca, the new village at the base of the mesa. Founded only about ten years before by Daisy's uncle, Tom Polacca, the village offered an easier life. Water bubbled from a nearby spring, and cottonwood trees growing along Polacca Wash shaded the children on hot days. The mesa top was barren—without trees, a blade of grass, or water. Everything had to be carried up on the backs of the people. In Polacca the family had things they needed close by, and there was a store there as well as a school.

Tom Polacca encouraged all of the Hopi children to attend the school and learn to speak English. The Tewa-Hopis of Hano agreed with him and willingly sent their children to school to learn the white people's way, but at that time, the Hopis of the other villages did not think it was necessary to learn English or white ways. Since the Tewa-Hopis had learned to speak English they began to serve as interpreters for the other Hopis. Tom Polacca went to Washington as a spokesperson for his people; later he was a leader and the Hopi interpreter for the government agency employees. The Tewa-Hopis had originally come as warriors to protect the Hopis on First Mesa; now they served as leaders in contact with the white people.

Daisy was eager to start school. She used to follow her sister, Rachel, to school. Even though she was too young to be enrolled, the teacher gave her paper and pencils and let her draw whatever she pleased while the other students studied their English lessons. After school Daisy followed Rachel to the field nurse's house. Daisy was only starting to learn English, but since the nurse spoke Tewa, they could talk with each other.

The following year, when she was seven, Daisy started school. She enjoyed being a real student at last, learning to count and to speak English.

CHAPTER III

Learning From Nampeyo

During the summer Willie and Annie sometimes had to go to the ranch to tend their cattle. While they were away, Daisy climbed the wagon road to Hano and stayed with Nampeyo.

Daisy always found her grandmother working with clay. Nampeyo sat on her blanket on the ground just outside the door of her house with everything she needed spread out before her. She could reach for her clay; a bowl with water for keeping her hands moist; a metate, the flat stone on which she ground the dry bee weed paint with another stone; and her polishing stones. She also had treats for the village children. She did not shoo them away when they huddled around to watch her make the pottery.

While she worked, she held the bowls up, turned them, and studied them from all sides. But she depended mostly on her hands to feel whether the bowl was evenly round. She used to tell Daisy that she could look way out beyond the edge of the mesa and still know if the pot was even or how thick the wall was.

Daisy wanted to roll the clay between her palms to make the coils for her own pots, but she did not want to waste Nampeyo's clay. Getting the clay ready for pottery making was a lot of hard work, and Daisy was afraid that her grandmother would scold her. The water that Nampeyo used to moisten the clay had been carried up on her back in a thin-necked pottery canteen. The heavy clay was dug out of the side of the mesa, and it, too, had to be carried up. The freshly dug clay had to be strained through a cloth to remove pebbles and bits of sticks. Then it was moistened with enough water to stick the particles together. Finally it was kneaded like bread until it was pliable enough to mold.

One day when Nampeyo went out to get some wood, Daisy pinched off a small piece of clay and went behind the stove. She made a ball, stuck her fingers in the middle, and began to shape a small bowl. She had no water, so she licked her finger with her tongue to keep the clay moist. Sometimes her fingerprints marked the clay, and she had to smooth them out. Other times the tiny pot bulged out on one side, and she had to try to push the bulge back into a perfectly round shape. She made several small pots and hid them all behind the stove.

A few days later, Nampeyo said that she was going to clean the house. Daisy watched her begin to sweep the room. She worked closer and closer to the stove. Then, with one wide motion of her arm, she swept under the stove, and Daisy's little bowls rolled out.

"What's this?" Nampeyo asked.

Daisy stood perfectly still, expecting to be scolded for wasting the good clay.

But Nampeyo was pleased. "You sit down with me and learn to make pottery," she said. Nampeyo told Daisy how she had learned to make pottery from her grandmother who had lived at Walpi, the Hopi village at the tip of First Mesa.

Nampeyo used to walk along the spine of the mesa through the village of Sichomovi to Walpi to visit her. When Nampeyo was a little girl, during the 1860s, the Hopi people at Walpi made the best pottery on First Mesa. It was a creamy yellow decorated in red and black. Although the Walpi pottery was not as beautiful as the pots made in the Hopi village of Sikyatki centuries before, the bowls were useful for cooking and storing food, and the ladles served the stew. It was all the people needed.

Nampeyo learned quickly and became such a skilled potter that even before she was twenty years old she was known as the best potter in Hano. She married Lesou, a man from Oraibi, a Hopi village on Third Mesa. When white people established stores on the reservation during the 1880s, Nampeyo sold her pottery decorated in the Walpi designs. She was able to sell all that she made at good prices because of the fine quality of her work. It helped support her family, and it helped the entire village. All of the families on the Hopi mesas shared food and helped one another. When the ceremonies were held, the women baked bread and made stews and sweet puddings. The prepared food, melons, and squash from the fields, and treats from the store were carried to the kiva during the ceremony. The men divided the food equally, even though some families brought more than others. In this way the extra things that Nampeyo could afford to bring were shared by the entire village.

Even after Nampeyo became a well-known potter, she lived like any other Tewa-Hopi in Hano, and shared what she had with others. But she also understood the importance of being able to earn her own living from pottery. Nampeyo

Nampeyo coiling a pot.

always told her daughters and granddaughters to learn to make good pottery so that they could support themselves.

After the day when Daisy's small bowls were discovered under the stove, she often sat beside her grandmother and made pottery. As Daisy shaped her small bowls, she held them up just as Nampeyo did. Daisy's were always lopsided.

"How can you get the even shape?" she asked.

"Your hand will tell you," Nampeyo said. "Your hand will tell you the shape of the pot."

After the pottery was formed and dried out in the sun, Nampeyo rubbed Daisy's bowls with her burnishing stone so that they would have a smooth surface and the walls would be an even thickness. Then she painted Daisy's little bowls and fired them with her own pottery. She took them to the store in Polacca and sold them with her own pots. When she returned, she had a penny for each tiny bowl. Very pleased with herself and with the money, Daisy bought some candy with it.

With practice, Daisy's hands became more skilled. As she learned to shape the bowls more evenly, she increased the size of the pottery. She started with a base shaped from a ball of clay, and then she built up the sides by adding coils of clay. The coils were pinched on around the rim of the bowl, and each coil had to be smoothed into it. In this way the walls grew higher and higher. Nampeyo thought Daisy learned very quickly. "Some day you will be like Nampeyo," she said.

During one of the times when Daisy stayed with Nampeyo, her grandmother took her to the Grand Canyon. Fred Harvey, who ran the shops and restaurants at the South Rim of the Grand Canyon, had invited Nampeyo to demonstrate pottery making for the tourists. He considered her the best potter in the Southwest.

Daisy's uncles took them to the train in a wagon. They teased Daisy when she squealed with excitement at the noisy, oncoming train. At the Grand Canyon she helped her grandmother. She felt proud to see all the people who came to see her grandmother work. Nampeyo showed them how she did everything from shaping the clay to firing the bowls. Since Nampeyo could speak only a few words of English, Daisy talked to the white people if they asked questions.

Daisy enjoyed going so far away from home and meeting so many different people. Nampeyo must have enjoyed her granddaughter's company, too, because she asked Daisy to go with her a second time. On this last visit to Grand Canyon, Daisy's parents came, and Annie painted designs on some of Nampeyo's pottery.

Daisy often went with her grandparents to the ruins of Sikyatki, which lies in the valley beside First Mesa. There they hunted for pieces of broken pottery. Sikyatki pottery had reached a peak of beauty before the village was suddenly abandoned in the sixteenth century. After that, the beauty of Hopi pottery had declined until Nampeyo revived the old Sikyatki designs. In later years, Nampeyo's daughters and granddaughters have continued to use the Sikyatki designs.

Daisy today shaping a pot with her hands.

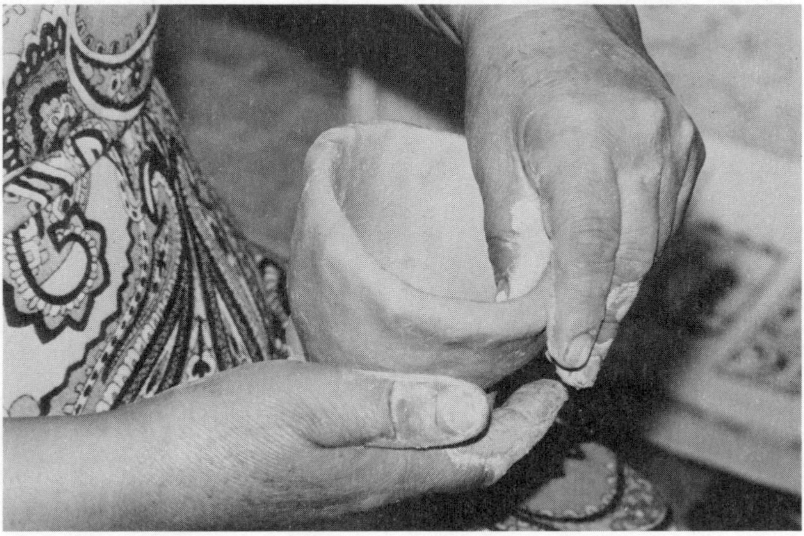

Daisy gathered the largest fragments she could find and dipped them into a pail of water to wash off the mud and sand. After the pieces had dried in the sun, the designs were as clear and bright as the day they were painted, some four hundred years before. Daisy's grandfather copied the designs on brown paper bags he had gotten at the store. When the bags were too big to use, Daisy hunted in the ruins until she found an arrowhead. Lesou used the sharp point to cut the paper. He said it was a good way to use arrowheads.

Daisy also looked for polishing stones that the people of Sikyatki had used to smooth their pottery. Because the stones had been rubbed over the rough clay so many times, they were as smooth and shiny as any machine could possibly polish them. Nampeyo liked to use the old stones, and she carried them with her whenever she demonstrated pottery making. Daisy still has two of these stones that her grandmother took to Chicago the year that Daisy was born. Daisy also found a clay whistle at Sikyatki, which the priests used during ceremonies. When Daisy raised it to her lips and blew, she heard the same reedy, birdlike call that had been heard centuries before in the kivas of Sikyatki.

As Nampeyo painted designs on her bowls, she told Daisy stories about the Hopi and Tewa people. Daisy listened with great interest to the legends of the creation of the people and the route of the clan migrations over the earth. Nampeyo also told her the story of the Tewas spitting into the pit, the symbolic way they buried their language. That was why Daisy and Nampeyo could speak Tewa and Hopi, but the people of Walpi and Sichomovi could speak only Hopi. Daisy has remembered the stories all of her life. They are more important to her than the things she learned in school, and even perhaps more important than the pottery making. The stories explained who the Hopi people were and why they lived in the Hopi Way.

As Daisy's skill in forming the small bowls and pots grew, she wanted to paint her own designs. But she had difficulty painting the straight lines that encircled the round bowls. The paint had to be applied correctly the first time. The dark brown pigment made from bee weed could not be erased or changed. Nampeyo told her that she was not holding the yucca fiber brush correctly. She put the brush between Daisy's thumb and index finger and anchored her last three fingers on the bowl. Then Nampeyo told Daisy to pull the brush over the bowl. That was all that Nampeyo ever taught Daisy about painting. "Put yourself on the bowl," Nampeyo said.

After the designs were painted on her bowls, Daisy wanted to learn how to fire her own pottery. But first Nampeyo and Lesou would only allow her to watch. Firing was the hardest part of pottery making. During this process, the bowls were most likely to break or be damaged by smoke.

Firing had to be done on a clear, windless day. The very early morning hours are about the only time the wind does not fiercely blow across First Mesa, so Daisy had to get up very early. It seemed to Daisy that firing took forever. The fire had to burn a certain length of time, or the pottery would not reach a temperature high enough to harden it and make it strong enough to use. When all that was left of the fire was a grey mound of ashes, Daisy wanted to pull out her pots.

"Just leave them alone," Nampeyo cautioned. If a breeze

hit the hot pottery, it would break. As last they hooked a stick into the necks of the pots and pulled them out of the ashes. When the beautiful brown and white pots were tapped on the ground to knock off the ashes, they rang as clear as a bell. This meant that the clay had actually changed its chemical composition from the heat of the fire and that it did not have cracks. Cracked pottery thudded dully. Nampeyo knew the pottery was sound and strong when it made that bell-like sound.

In this way Daisy learned her art from Nampeyo from the time she was seven until she was about ten years old. She learned a traditional craft that is older than the history of her people. In fact, what we know of their history is written in the broken pieces of pottery, so the pottery itself becomes their history. Throughout the centuries, the craft of pottery has been passed from mother to daughter and granddaughter in the way that Daisy learned pottery making from Nampeyo.

CHAPTER IV

From Darkness To The City Of Light

Daisy loved school. Her teacher recognized Daisy's talent in art and encouraged her to draw, just as Nampeyo encouraged her to make pottery. But after Daisy had been going to school for about two years, she began to have difficulty seeing the crayon marks well enough to draw. When she worked on pottery, she could no longer paint straight lines. Her parents treated her eyes with blue stone medicine, a Hopi remedy for eye infections. It hurt so much that Daisy cried and cried.

When she was about ten years old, her brothers and some friends were scheduled to go to the Indian school in Phoenix. Even though Daisy was having difficulty seeing and she was too young for the boarding school, she wanted to go with them. She did not want to be left out, and she was eager for as much education as she could get. She pleaded with her parents until they signed a special paper, and she was allowed to go.

Daisy's eyesight grew worse at boarding school. When she tried to do mathematics, the three looked like a five and the five like a three. She told the teacher that she had to sit at the front. Still she made mistakes. The teacher did not understand that she gave the wrong answers simply because she could not see. One day she became so impatient that she hit Daisy with a long ruler. Hopi children are not often punished by whippings. Daisy remembers the incident so vividly that she still raises her hand protectively to her head when she tells the story today.

One day Daisy was called out of the class to see a visitor. The principal from the school at Polacca had come to visit the children from the village. Daisy was pleased to see someone from home. When she told him about her eye trouble, he took her home.

Back in Polacca, Daisy went to school every day until the bright Arizona sunshine hurt her eyes so much that she could no longer go outdoors. Finally she could not even stand to be in a room without a cover over the window. Even a pinpoint of light hurt her eyes. Her parents applied the painful blue stone, but nothing helped. She spent all of her time in a completely darkened room. It was a lonely place.

One day a stranger came to visit Daisy. She put her arms around the little girl and said that it was a great pity for Daisy to stay by herself in the dark. She asked Daisy if she would like to go to California and have her sight restored with an operation. Cataracts had formed in Daisy's eyes as a result of infection. The lens of the eye had turned cloudy, and it was necessary to remove the lens in order for her to see again. Daisy was not certain if she wanted to go or not, but she realized that without surgery, she would soon be blind. She wanted to be able to make pottery with Nampeyo again. She wanted to go back to school and to play in the sunshine. After thinking it over carefully, Daisy agreed to the operation.

Daisy's visitor was Anita Baldwin, a wealthy woman from California who often used her money to help others. Anita had come to Polacca to study Hopi music and customs, and she was camping in Willie's peach orchard with a group of friends when she found out about Daisy's blindness. After she had talked with Daisy, she spent a long time with Daisy's parents, discussing the plans they would make. Anita told Willie and Annie that they would hear from her soon.

Not long after Anita Baldwin had gone back to California, the superintendent of Polacca brought a letter from her and money for Daisy's family. The Healings began to get Daisy ready at once. They took her shopping for new clothes and packed her bags. Before Daisy could finish her breakfast the next morning, it was time to go to the train. She rode all by herself from Arizona to southern California. She was eleven years old and nearly blind.

At the moment she boarded the train, Daisy entered a way of life very different from the one she had shared with her family at Black Mesa—the life of the very rich. She rode in a private car that belonged to Anita Baldwin. After a day and a night the train stopped just for Daisy in Arcadia, a town near Los Angeles. The station had been built by Anita Baldwin's father for his own use, and the town had grown up around the station. When Daisy stepped off the train, a chauffeur slipped her into a Rolls Royce for the ride to Anoakia, the Baldwin estate.

Anita Baldwin was the daughter of E. J. Baldwin, or Lucky, as he was always called. It was a fitting nickname. Lucky Baldwin had come to California in 1853 in a covered wagon, and nearly every business he took up after that time turned out to be very profitable. When he died, Anita inherited silver mines, gold mines, and several ranches in southern California where oil was discovered. Anita also inherited her father's love for racehorses. So great was her love for horses that Anita directed the stable to be built first when she planned Anoakia on the Santa Anita ranch. She lived in the stable for several months in order to supervise building of the main house. It was her wish to make Santa Anita a prize ranch where the finest livestock grazed on the rolling hills, and fruits of many varieties grew in the orchards. Years later she built the Santa Anita racetrack where horse races are held to this day.

Within a few days after Daisy arrived at Anoakia, she was sent to a hospital in Los Angeles for eye surgery. After the cataracts were removed, she had to wear bandages over her eyes for about ten days. The bandages began to itch, but she was told that she must not touch them. Finally, the doctor came and unwound the bandages. She looked out of the window. She could see a tree clearly, and birds flitting in the branches. Everything seemed brighter and bigger than she remembered. She thought that it was a dream, and she was afraid that she would wake up in dimness again. But when she woke up the next morning, the trees and birds were just as bright and clear. Daisy was so excited and happy to see again that tears flooded her eyes.

Soon after the bandages were removed, Daisy returned to Anita Baldwin's home. With her restored eyesight, she discovered the vastness and wealth of Anoakia, located on the eight thousand-acre Santa Anita Ranch. Peacocks strutted in gardens crowded with eucalyptus and palm trees. It seemed like a jungle compared to the dry desert brush of

Black Mesa. Inside the mansion, Daisy found murals painted by the western artist Maynard Dixon in the enormous Indian Hall. Stretching to a length of eighteen feet, the murals pictured different aspects of Indian life in western settings. Anita Baldwin was very interested in painting and American Indian life, and she generously supported both interests.

Daisy stayed at Anoakia for several years, and she enrolled in high school in Pasadena. At school Daisy did work with clay again, but it was commercial clay, bought from an art store, and the pottery was made with molds or on a potter's wheel. Daisy showed the other students how to make pots in the old way, using coils of clay to build up the sides and using her hands to feel the shape and to mold round, even pots. Everyone at school was amazed that she could make such perfectly round pots without using a spinning potter's wheel or a mold.

Her art teacher arranged some apples and grapes on a

Anoakia, Anita Baldwin's beautiful home in California, where Daisy stayed for several years.

table. They reflected in the shiny surface. Daisy painted a still life of the reflected fruit. The teacher thought so highly of the painting that she sent it to Europe along with some of Daisy's coiled pottery to be exhibited with other students' art work. Daisy also painted a picture of a Hopi girl wearing her hair brushed into squash blossom coils above each ear. Daisy explained to the teacher that Hopi girls are considered old enough to marry when they reach puberty. As a sign that they are of marrying age, one of the older women in the girl's family brushes her hair over a flat U-shaped stick. When the stick is slipped out, the hair is pinned above each ear. These circles represent squash blossoms. Daisy had brought the ways of the desert to her California schoolroom and made them come alive in her art work.

Daisy's life was a pattern of vivid contrasts during her early teenage years. During the school year she lived with Anita Baldwin, but each summer she returned to Polacca to visit her family. The way she was treated as an individual and praised for her artistic talent at school probably affected her more than any of the luxuries she enjoyed at Anoakia. The Hopi do not praise or reward individuals for their accomplishments, and a person's standing in the community depends on his or her clan membership rather than on personal achievement. Since Hopi society depends on sharing and working together, competition and personal ambition are looked on with disapproval.

A sculptor, Emry Kopta, was living in Polacca during the time of Daisy's summer visits. Daisy showed him some of the paintings she had done in California. Impressed, he told her that she ought to study sculpture. He wrote a letter to Anita Baldwin in which he explained that he thought

The squash blossom hairstyle that Daisy used in her painting and later, in her stone carving.

Daisy was talented and that she ought to have more intense art study.

After reading Kopta's letter and talking to Daisy's teachers, Anita Baldwin decided to take Daisy to Europe with her and enroll her in L'École des Beaux Arts, or the School of Fine Arts, in Paris. When Daisy first heard about Paris, she was not sure if it was another town in California or exactly where it was. When she learned that it was in

Europe and that the people who lived in France spoke another language, she accepted the challenge. She had already learned to live with people who spoke a language she had learned only after she started school. The opportunity to go to a fine arts school appealed to her more than the idea of learning a new language frightened her.

When Daisy arrived in Paris, Anita Baldwin left her to travel through Europe while Daisy studied. Daisy did not speak a single word of French, and she lived with an older woman who did not speak a single word of English. Daisy listened to records and started to pick up a few words in the new language. At first the days seemed long in a strange place with another language to learn. Daisy lost count of the days and had no idea how many weeks she would have to spend in Paris by herself. It was not long, however, before she could speak French well enough to chat and joke with the other students at the art school. Everyone was very friendly.

Each morning the French woman fixed her breakfast, and then Daisy set out on the streets of Paris to go to L'École des Beaux Arts. Located on the River Seine that cuts through the heart of the city, the Beaux Arts is the finest art school in Paris.

Wearing a mask so that the stone chips would not fly into her eyes, Daisy spent her mornings chiseling stone in sculpture class. One large project that she completed early in the course was a bust of Moses with a beard and hair curling about his face.

Besides sculpture, Daisy studied painting. When she wanted to relax, she did pencil drawings. Returning to her room at the end of the day, she walked along the buildings in the soft grey atmosphere of Paris, the City of Light. Each time she passed the entrance to a courtyard, she could smell the mildew odor of old, wet stone. The cobbles were worn where first horses and now automobiles carried people in and out of the courtyards. Paris was as strange to her at first as the palatial Baldwin home had been. But in her quiet way, Daisy adapted again and added new skills to her artistic ability. She found the classes at Beaux Arts far more difficult than those at the school in Pasadena, and she worried that she would not pass. But at the end of her formal art studies, she was awarded a certificate that declared she was a graduate of L'École des Beaux Arts.

One exciting event happened while she studied in Paris. Charles Lindbergh landed there after the first nonstop flight from New York over the Atlantic Ocean. Daisy remembers the period when she was in Paris as the time when Lindbergh landed, not as the year 1927. Daisy measures her life in terms of events, not of dates. All of the dates used in this story of her life, and even her own age, are told as she tries to remember them now. Since she attaches little importance to dates, they are only approximate. It is the event itself that lives vividly in Daisy's memory.

When Daisy finished her studies, Anita Baldwin had returned to Paris. Now it seemed to Daisy that the time at Beaux Arts had gone very quickly. Deciding that Daisy ought to see and study sculpture in other places, Anita took her on a journey around the world. Anita had traveled widely throughout her life, so for her the trip was not unusual. They went to Switzerland, Germany, Italy, and Austria. In Florence, Italy, Daisy studied marble statues of the Renaissance and in Vienna the baroque style of architecture.

They traveled to Spain, where Daisy and Anita were presented to Queen Victoria Eugenia Cristina. They braved the heat of North Africa and then shivered in the cold northern climate of Finland and Russia. Great Buddhas towered over them in the temples of China.

Finally, after many months of travel, they returned to California. Daisy was about twenty years old, scarcely older than a high school graduate, but she was far more mature than her years would indicate. Daisy had known pain and endured blindness, she was skilled in several arts, and she had enjoyed the richness and variety of experience that travel can bring.

CHAPTER V

Home To The Hopi Way

Very soon after returning to California, Daisy went back to Polacca to visit her family. It had been a long time since her last visit; she had traveled far and seen many things during the period that she had been away from the wind-swept desert plain. Everyone wanted to know about her adventures. Very few of the people had traveled beyond the Hopi grazing lands that lay just beyond the squash fields at the base of the mesa.

One of the people Daisy saw again was a young Tewa-Hopi, Ray Naha, who had attended Polacca Day School with her. One evening his family brought a cow they had slaughtered as a gift to Daisy's family. It was an important gift, a sign that they wanted the young people to marry. Exchange of lavish gifts between the families and clans of the young people is part of the Hopi marriage ritual. Daisy did not know what to do. She had been invited to dinner at the home of the superintendent of Polacca that same evening, so she decided to go to dinner and put off the problem. It was very late when she returned, but Ray was waiting for her.

Daisy was very uncomfortable. To amuse him, she told him about all of the places she had visited around the world.

She told him about living in Paris, and before that, about living with Anita Baldwin at Anoakia. Finally, she had to talk to him about getting married. She told him that she did not feel ready. The Hopi Way was for a girl to know how to do everything before she was married. During their teenage years, Hopi girls stayed very close to home. They did all of the household tasks throughout the year with their mothers. In that way they learned how to cook, how to plaster adobe walls, and how to dig, sift, and paint whitewash. They also helped their mothers care for the younger children in the family. If they had older married sisters, they helped care for their nephews and nieces.

Even if Daisy had gone to the Indian boarding school in Phoenix, she would have come home and learned all of these things in the proper time from her mother. But she had been away, living in the white world for nearly ten years. She was not prepared to be a married Hopi woman. Ray understood. He said that Daisy's family could keep the cow, but he would not expect her to marry him.

After her visit home, Daisy went back to California for a short period. She stayed in a Baldwin Hotel at Lake Tahoe, high in the mountains. After helping there for awhile, she intended to go back to Pasadena and continue her art studies. Before enrolling in school, she visited her family in Polacca again.

She noticed that Annie, her mother, seemed to be coughing and that she needed to rest more than usual. Annie had never been strong and had never been able to make as much pottery as her sisters. Daisy realized that her mother was getting old. If Daisy kept going away, her family would not know her anymore. It was time for Daisy to choose between living in the white world or being a Hopi.

She chose to stay with her family. She felt deep gratitude to Anita Baldwin for her kindness and generosity. Daisy never forgot the fact that she would still be sitting in a darkened room if Anita had not rescued her. Her chance to study sculpture in Paris and to travel around the world was Anita Baldwin's gift. Daisy kept in contact with her, and years after Anita Baldwin's death, Daisy visited her son at his home in Pasadena.

Not long after she returned to Polacca she met Ray Naha again at the store. The store served as a meeting place for the people from First Mesa. They did not go there just to buy groceries, but they always stayed and exchanged news with Hopis from other villages. Those who had moved down to Polacca kept up with happenings on the mesa top. The store was their telephone and their newspaper.

When Daisy saw Ray again, she found that he was still interested in her. They talked for a long time, and when they discussed getting married, Daisy agreed. Now the time was right to turn her back on art studies and to start the life of a Hopi wife.

Living again among her mother and sisters, Daisy naturally picked up clay and began to coil pottery. Nampeyo, in spite of growing old and losing her eyesight, continued to make pottery. While Daisy was away, the shapes of Nampeyo's pots had gradually changed. Now she formed nearly all of the pots with a wide shoulder, just like the Sikyatki pottery. When Nampeyo had started to use the Sikyatki designs on her pottery, she had painted the designs on bowls and pots that were shaped like Walpi pottery her grandmother had made. Gradually, she began to make the shoulders flatter and wider, like the shape of the Sikyatki pots. This flat wide portion provided a wide surface for painting the designs. One of Nampeyo's favorites was an eagle pattern in which round, curving lines and straight, geometric features curved down from the neck of the pot to just below the wide surface of the shoulder. The painted design harmonized perfectly with the shape of the bowl.

One of the beauties of Nampeyo's pottery was that although she used old designs and shapes, she never copied the old pottery detail for detail. She used it in her own way, and her daughters and granddaughters followed her example. They all used the Sikyatki designs, but each of them added their own individual touches. Daisy's designs were slightly different from her sister Rachel's, and each time that Daisy painted one of the old designs, she tended to arrange the design on the pot in a slightly new way, so that each pot varied from those created before.

After Daisy returned to First Mesa, she noticed changes. Except for Nampeyo, most of her family had moved down to Polacca. The village men often worked for wages at the government agency at Keams Canyon or on projects like the big dams. This changed the old pattern of food and service exchanges and the importance of clans in family life. Another change was that more women besides the relatives of Nampeyo had taken up pottery making for sale.

When Daisy was a child, all of the women made pottery, but only for storing corn, carrying water, or for cooking. Sturdy and adequate for these purposes, the pottery was not beautifully decorated or evenly shaped. It would not have appealed to white people to buy, so the traders paid little for it. Later the women found they could buy inexpensive kettles and pots at the store, and they nearly stopped making pottery. But when they realized that Nampeyo earned a living income from her pottery, they decided to make it to sell to the traders. During Nampeyo's life no one ever equalled her skill or achieved her fame, but the financial lot of many families on First Mesa improved because of the income from pottery making. Daisy's grandmother can be credited with this revival.

As Nampeyo's sight failed, she could no longer see well enough to paint the designs on her pots. The traders were still interested in her work and told her to continue to form the pots and have someone else paint them. Lesou helped her paint until his death in 1932. After that Nampeyo used to walk down the path from the top of the mesa carrying the unpainted pots in a bag. She brought them to Daisy and to Daisy's aunt, Fannie, who also lived in Polacca. When Daisy and Fannie painted her pots, they signed Nampeyo's name and their own at the bottom. Eventually Nampeyo lost her sight entirely, and she became known as the Blind Potter of Hano. Even so she could form pots that were almost perfectly round. Her hands continued to work with the clay and tell her the shape of the pot.

And then even Nampeyo's hands failed her as she became more feeble and then childlike. During the last few years of her life, she sat on her bed in her room and played with things given to her. Children continued to love her as they had long ago when she sat at her door and gave them candy.

Nampeyo died in 1942. But the skill of her eyes, and her hands, and her spirit lives in the beautiful creamy white, tan, and brown pottery displayed in museums all over the United States.

Daisy decorates the pots as Nampeyo checks them for roundness. Daisy's son, Ray, sits quietly.

After Daisy and Ray married, they had their own stone and adobe house in Polacca. Like other Hopi women, Daisy did housework and prepared meals in addition to making pottery. When her first child, Ray, was born, there was a baby on a cradle board to be taken care of and to be carried around when she had to leave the house. Daisy found each new homemaking responsibility difficult. Perhaps if she had learned how to take care of a house and babies instead of studying art for ten years, she could have managed more easily. But it seemed that new tasks were thrust upon her before she had learned how to take care of the old ones. Not long after Ray left the cradle board, a daughter, Shirley, was born. Daisy had made the choice to return to her people, but the life of a Hopi woman was sometimes too much for her to handle. She had been away so long that it no longer seemed natural to her.

Besides caring for her house and family and making pottery, Daisy belonged to a religious organization in Hano and participated in all of their dances and ceremonies. Whatever changes the outside world brought to First Mesa, the ceremonies and dances still held great importance for the people. Sometimes changes were made, but the ceremonies still went on. Most of the kachina dances were now held on Saturday night so that people who worked away from First Mesa could return over the weekend for the dances. One of the clans in Hano died out, but another that claimed to be related to it took over its ceremonies. Protestant missions were established in Polacca, but they did not attract many converts or affect the religious life in the kivas on the mesa top.

Busy as she was, Daisy found the time to take advantage of an unusual opportunity in 1935 when staff members of the Peabody Museum of Harvard University came to Awatovi to excavate its ruins. Awatovi, the village totally destroyed by the Hopis in 1700 when Catholic missionaries had tried to rebuild a church there, was on Antelope Mesa, about fifteen miles east of Polacca. Nampeyo and Lesou had been there years before, sifting through the sand to look for potsherds. When the archeologists dug into the ruins, they uncovered whole pots.

Daisy liked the busy, but orderly digging. She noticed how carefully the archeologists treated the remnants of pottery, rotted timbers of buried houses, and tumbled stones. They brushed everything with soft brushes, measured the objects, and sometimes photographed items before they removed them. Later everything was labeled.

Spending the night when she went there, Daisy got up at sunrise and sat sketching the designs of the ancient people until sundown when darkness prevented her from drawing any longer. The archeologists were interested in her pottery making in the old way, and they questioned her about each part of the process.

Daisy's skill at drawing, a natural talent improved by her studies in California and Paris, was a great asset in copying the designs accurately. When she had copied all that she wanted from Awatovi, she had a stack of papers as thick as a book. She treasured those designs that she herself discovered. She painted some on her own pottery; she gave others to her sisters. Other potters on First Mesa passed them around and began to use her drawings to put Awatovi designs on their pots. In this way, Daisy contributed to the revival of Hopi pottery, just as Nampeyo had inspired women to go back to the old shapes and designs. In time the original drawings were lost, but even without them, Daisy still paints some Awatovi designs on her pots, for they are engraved in her memory.

The burdens of Daisy's home life continued to grow and demand more of her attention. Although she spent much

A storage pot made by Daisy.

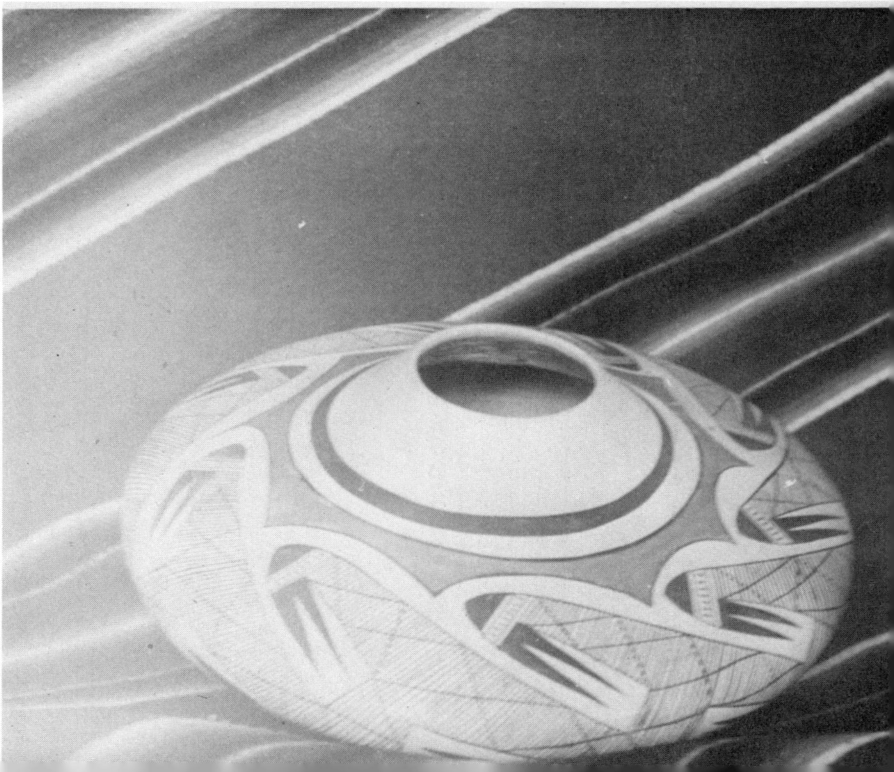

time with her sister Rachel, working with clay, most of her time and energy had to be spent keeping house and taking care of little Ray and Shirley. Near the end of the 1930s another baby, Louella, was born. Like Daisy's father, Ray Naha kept cattle at a ranch. When he needed to tend the cattle, Daisy went with him to the ranch. There she prepared the meals for the men who worked with the cattle. It seemed that she scarcely had breakfast cleaned up before it was time to cook a hearty midday meal. Then at the end of the day, the hungry work crew had to be fed again. For Daisy, who felt that she never really had learned how to care for a house or to cook, it was even more difficult to cook for so many people away from her own stove and the convenience of her own kitchen. At one period she became ill and entered the hospital at Keams Canyon. The doctor felt that she suffered from nothing else than the strain of working too hard.

Perhaps the hard work and her many responsibilities would have been easier for her to handle if she had been happy in her marriage, but she felt that her husband sometimes treated her badly. After one especially unhappy incident, in which her pride was deeply hurt, she took the two young children and the baby on the cradle board and went back to live in her mother's house. She and Ray were divorced.

She told her mother that now she would learn the things she would have learned before her marriage if she had stayed in Polacca. Maybe by working each day beside Annie, Daisy would better understand what she needed to do to keep the house and to raise her children in the Hopi Way.

CHAPTER VI

A New Pueblo And New Skills

While Daisy was living with her parents after the divorce, some of their friends from Zuni Pueblo in western New Mexico came to visit. They invited Daisy to return to Zuni with them to watch Shalako, the most festive and important of all Zuni ceremonies.

The midwinter festival is dominated by the Shalakos, representatives of the gods who come to visit Zuni from their sacred world. Symbolically, the six Shalakos—one for each of the six Zuni kivas—and their attendants trace the wanderings of the Zunis from creation to the present Zuni world. Six to eight houses are especially built or completely remodeled to honor them. In turn, each Shalako and two groups of the attendants spend the night blessing a house and offering prayers to insure fertility, long life, prosperity, and happiness. To the desert-dwelling Zunis this means rain.

Preparation begins in January in the kivas and other sacred places and with the building of the Shalako houses. The men who are chosen to represent the Shalakos and other attendants learn the dances and chants and help build the houses. The activity reaches a climax on Shalako Day when the costumed, masked gods appear at the village about dusk. And indeed, they appear to have come from

A painting of Hopi Shalakos by Otis Polelonema.

another world. Standing ten feet tall, the Shalakos lean slightly forward and move in a swaying walk. Their brightly decorated white costumes are topped with a colorful turquoise mask, which is surrounded by a ruff of eagle feathers at the throat and a fanned headpiece. Two horns jut out from the sides, enormous eyes stare blindly ahead, and a wooden beak clacks at certain parts in the ceremony. All of this magic is created by a man who walks concealed in the long costume and carries the mask on a pole.

Daisy enjoyed watching the Shalako ceremony and forgot her own personal unhappiness in the holiday atmosphere. She stayed in Zuni until the peach trees bloomed in the spring.

A short time later, Daisy married Leo Poblano, whom she had come to know during her long stay in Zuni. She left Polacca to live in Zuni Pueblo, where the houses are as red as the sandstone of Zuni Sacred Mountain that towers above the plain four miles away. Unlike the bare mesas of the Hopi villages, Zuni is cupped in a gentle valley along the Zuni River. Pines grow on the hills, and cottonwoods line the river bank. The countryside is less harsh than the high, wind-blown desert plain of Daisy's childhood.

It was 1939, and Daisy's youngest child was still small

Zuni Pueblo. The round structures in front of the church are ovens for baking bread.

enough to swing on a cradle board. Leo was a kind man, and he treated Daisy's three children as though they were his own. As the seasons passed and as one Shalako after another was celebrated, Leo and Daisy never had any children of their own, but the five of them were a happy family.

Leo was one of the best silversmiths in Zuni, which is famous for its silversmiths. Cut and polished stones, set or inlaid on silver in complicated patterns are Zuni specialties. Leo taught Daisy how to do inlay work, using turquoise, jet, coral, and shell. After cutting and polishing flat pieces and chips of stone, they fitted them together like the pieces of a puzzle to form geometric patterns on top of the silver.

Daisy liked to work with the silver and stones, and she learned quickly. But as she remembers, most of the silversmiths who worked with inlay created two patterns over and over. They were the curved rainbow god and the knife-wing god, sometimes called a thunderbird. Daisy wanted to change that. She began to create new designs and instead of cutting and polishing a flat surface on the stones, she carved features in relief. Her training in sculpture at L' École des Beaux Arts had prepared her for relief stone carving. Her adventurous spirit prompted her to try something new.

Daisy's first original design was a large inlay of a Hopi girl that she mounted on the cover of a silver jewelry box. The Hopi girl with the squash blossom hairstyle, a figure she had often used in her art classes at school, was one of her favorite subjects. Daisy cut the girl's hair from jet. Carving eyes, nose, and mouth into a small piece of brown shell demanded steady hands, but the finished face looked like a miniature sculpture in relief, rather than a single flat piece of stone. Daisy fitted tiny strips of silver over the girl's

Carvings and jewelry by Leo Poblano.

arm for bracelets, set in a red stone for her dress, and a black jet for the manta, or shawl, that Hopi women wrap under arm and draw over the the opposite shoulder. Leo was so impressed that he began to do relief carving also. They were the first artists in Zuni to do such figures. Daisy's impulse to create something new and to change the old style added a fresh dimension to Zuni silverwork. It added to the reputation of the Zuni silversmiths.

Daisy also carved one of the dancers from the Shalako ceremony in inlay. Soon after she finished, some of the priests came to see her and told her that she could not make the Shalako figures because she was Hopi, not Zuni. She explained that she had found the figures pictured in a book. The Shalakos were no longer a secret—people all over the world knew about them. She told the Zuni priests that their ancestors should have sat on their secrets, but instead they put them out like food on the table for anyone to take. Even though her arguments seemed reasonable to her, Daisy could not change the priests' minds. They took the book away from her, and she did not carve the Shalako figures anymore.

In the early 1940s large pieces of turquoise were still available in the mines of Arizona, Colorado, and Nevada. Daisy and Leo sculpted free-standing figures out of these large stones. When she picked up one of the rough chunks, Daisy could imagine the hidden figure. The shape of the stone always suggested the shape of something waiting to be set free. One mine-rough piece looked like a Navajo woman. Daisy picked up her chisels and chipped and carved the Navajo, wearing a full skirt, fringed shawl, and holding a baby on a cradle board. After it was carved and polished, the rough stone became a smooth statue.

A carving of a Navajo woman and child by Daisy.

Daisy also carved a Zuni woman grinding corn and another figure holding a loaf of Pueblo bread. In the second carving, Daisy dared to carve a hole between the woman's arm and her body. It was risky because the slender arm could easily break off while she carved out the space. But the arm withstood the stress, and the figure stood with a natural space between the arm and body.

Daisy and Leo sold or traded all of their work at this time to C. G. Wallace, an Indian trader who lived at Zuni. He had a store where he sold groceries and tools needed to tend the fields and keep the houses. He supplied the Zunis with silver, turquoise, and other stones for their jewelry and turquoise figures. Then he paid them for their work, often in food or other items. Daisy and Leo were frequently paid with second-hand furniture. Wallace sold the Zuni jewelry and carvings to shops all over the Southwest. He sold Daisy's jewelry box with the Hopi girl to Maisels, a shop in Albuquerque. For years the box was displayed in a showcase. Whenever Daisy went to Albuquerque, she went into the shop to see it. One day she discovered that it was gone. She learned that it had been sold, but there was no record of the buyer's name. The person who bought it had no idea who created it because, at that time, the Zunis did not sign their work. Daisy felt as if the box had been lost.

Many items that Daisy and Leo sold to C. G. Wallace stayed in his collection, since he kept his favorite pieces. In time the collection grew to become one of the largest and most famous Indian jewelry and gem collections in the United States. Fortunately, Wallace cataloged all of the things he kept, so that the artist is known. Many years later, when the collection was auctioned, the catalog showed that he had kept thirty pieces by Leo and four by Daisy. Several of his carvings by Leo and Daisy were given to the Heard Museum in Phoenix where they may be seen today.

After Daisy settled in Zuni, she built a new house large enough for the family. As she shaped the walls of her house with the red stones and adobe mud of Zuni, she arranged the rooms as she wanted them. Instead of a full wall between the kitchen and living room, she built the partition only waist high so that she could see into both rooms when she prepared meals. In time running water and electricity were put into the house. Fragrant juniper and piñon fires in the stove warmed the house in winter. In the spring the peach tree bloomed, and Daisy planted beans, squash, and peppers in her garden. In the fall Daisy strung the peppers into ristras and hung them outside the kitchen window. As they dried, they turned a brilliant deep red.

Daisy's three children, Ray, Shirley, and Louella, attended school in Zuni. Ray showed a talent for drawing just as Daisy had when she was a student. During these busy years of running a household and working as a silversmith and sculptor in turquoise, Daisy still helped support the family by working in the home of one of the traders who lived in Zuni. In those days, the return in money or goods to the Indian artists was small. The crafts did not command the prices they do now. The system of selling to a trader, who sold to a dealer, who then sold to the public, brought very little to the original artist. Today many of the successful Indian artists sell directly to collectors. Craft cooperatives and guilds, run by the craftsmen themselves, also insure decent prices for the Indian artist. But many men and women still sell their pottery, jewelry, and rugs through the system of traders and dealers.

Although Daisy enjoyed carving the figures out of turquoise, she eventually found it difficult to get pieces large enough to carve a figure. By the end of the 1940s only small stones suitable for setting into jewelry or for carving tiny animal figures were available. Daisy carved some of these figures, which are often strung on necklaces with turquoise or coral beads. Then she decided to give up stone carving, and she went back to making Hopi pottery. Never again did she pick up the chisel and carving tools to make jewelry or statues.

For about ten years Daisy had practiced a new art. Just as it is unusual for Pueblo artists to try new designs and ideas, it is unusual for them to change from one art form to the other. But Daisy had successfully mastered both stone carving and pottery making. The best of her pottery was still ahead of her.

CHAPTER VII

A Potter Again

After Daisy decided to return to pottery making, she hunted for clay beds around Zuni, sometimes walking fifteen miles in one day. Daisy found some clay, but she discovered that it was grey and sticky. She preferred the Hopi clay, the surface of which fired to a creamy yellow color, and so she devoted most of her time to making pottery in the Hopi style with clay she brought from First Mesa.

After she had made several of the Hopi pots, she suggested to Leo that he could make a silver bowl shaped like pottery. They carved a large block of wood into the shape of the bowl. Then Leo covered the entire bowl with silver plate and soldered the seams together. He decorated the silver bowl with turquoise. They were both proud of the new idea.

Leo was a fine father to the children and a good companion for Daisy. Working together added to their marriage. Instead of Leo's going off every day to a job while Daisy stayed at home, they both worked as artists and shared that part of their life, too.

Besides being silversmiths, Zuni men earned fame for their fire fighting skill. Throughout the dry late summer and early fall, they often traveled far from Zuni to fight fires in the tinder dry forests of the West. One summer in the late 1950s Leo went with a band of Zuni firefighters to California. They were gone many days, but that was not unusual since great fires sometimes raged through the canyons for a week or more. Leo was not with the men when they finally returned. They told Daisy that he had been killed by a falling tree. Even though Daisy grieved for her husband, she continued to coil her pots as usual. She still had her work—and her children, of whom she was very proud.

Daisy's children were growing up and leaving the stone and adobe house. Ray, who had shown promise as an artist in the school in Zuni, had gone on to study at Sherman Institute in Riverside, California. After he had finished his formal training, he went to the Hopi village of Oraibi and studied with Fred Kabotie, a well-known Hopi painter. He later made his home in San Carlos, Arizona, not far from Zuni.

Whenever Ray visited Daisy, he constantly sketched her or anyone else he talked to. His restless hands captured people on the pages of his sketchbook. He sold his paintings to galleries in Phoenix and Scottsdale. As his reputation grew, reproductions of his work appeared in books about Indian artists. His paintings were exhibited in San Francisco. And then, in midcareer, Ray died suddenly when he was about forty-five years old. Naturally, it was a tragic blow to Daisy, but she takes some comfort in the fact that her daughter, Shirley, still has many of Ray's largest paintings.

Shirley became a silversmith like her stepfather. When she married, she moved to Gallup, only a few miles from

Zuni. Then Louella married and moved to Los Angeles, too far for Daisy to see her very often.

When Daisy was lonely, she went back to First Mesa to visit her sister, Rachel, and her brothers. She watched the work of Rachel's four daughters, who were all active potters.

Daisy and her sister also discovered that their reputations were growing. Instead of having to take their pottery to the trader to sell, the traders came to them, asking for their pots. In time, the collectors themselves began to come to their homes to buy the pottery. Eventually they sold most of their work this way. They prefer to sell directly to people. Today the best way to buy pottery from Daisy or Rachel is to visit them at their homes in Zuni or Polacca.

After a time, Daisy married Sidney Hooee, and he came to live with her in the house that she had built. Like so many Zunis, Sidney is also a fine silversmith. He specializes in channel work, inlaying the well-polished stones between fine lines of silver, or "channels." Some of his wide bracelets have four rows of polished stones set in the silver channels. People travel many miles to buy the bracelets they have ordered from him.

As the years passed and Daisy's reputation grew, Sidney often sat beside her at interviews or pottery demonstrations. But being a very quiet man, he remained silent as Daisy did all the storytelling, gesturing, and explaining.

During the 1960s, Daisy became so well known that she could have spent all of her time making bowls and pots to fill orders for collectors of her work, but she felt a responsibility for passing the tradition on to others. The Zuni women had been expert potters, making beautiful water

Daisy and Sidney working in their home in Zuni.

jars, or ollas, that they carried on their heads. But now pottery making was nearly a dead art in the village. Whenever tourists visited the pueblo, they asked where they could buy pottery. There never was any pottery to buy; the Zunis made only jewelry.

Daisy began to teach pottery making at the high school. She encouraged her students to make Zuni ollas. When she taught pottery making to the Zuni girls, she could tell them how to coil and shape the wet clay into the typical olla shape, but she never taught them exactly how to paint the designs on the water jars. She told her students they had to study the old designs and then put them on the pots themselves. This is a typical pattern in passing the tradition of pottery from one person to another. Methods for working and shaping the clay are carefully explained and demonstrated, but learning to paint the designs is a skill that each potter learns for herself.

Zunis often paint a rain bird, a simple design formed by curving lines. Other designs are a sunflower and the Zuni deer. The designs are painted in dark brown bee weed and a yellow clay that turns red when the olla is fired. The white background comes from several coats of white slip—runny clay that is painted over the grey pots. Daisy sometimes makes the ollas and paints Zuni designs on them; they are prized by collectors and are quickly bought.

Zuni girls carry the ollas on their heads in the Inter-tribal Ceremonies held in Gallup every August. Perfect posture and smooth movements are necessary to carry the jars without accident. Each Indian tribe shows off its skills at the Inter-tribals, so the Zuni girls try to perfect their marching. Each year before the ceremonials, the girls come to Daisy's house to practice. Although Daisy is a Hopi woman, she teaches the girls to sing and to balance the jars on their heads.

When Daisy taught in the high school, she noticed that the students were eager to learn, but then, after graduation, they often moved away to take city jobs. Away from the source of clay and without the inspiration of their teacher, their skill was forgotten and lost.

To try to reach more people in the pueblo, Daisy runs a workshop in her home for Zuni women. The pottery offers the women a source of income, and Daisy hopes that it will add to the revival of Zuni pottery. She expects that these women will in turn teach their own children and grandchildren. Many of these women have their grandchildren

Daisy with one of her pots.

living with them while their daughters and sons work. This is a common pattern. In the old days, the young parents worked with livestock, and Daisy spent so much time with Nampeyo because her parents were often at the ranch. Now the young people usually work in nearby cities, so that the rearing of young children often falls to grandparents as it did in the old days.

In recent years, Daisy has noticed that people from the pueblo have begun to order the old traditional ceremonial bowls and jars. Although the cycle of religious ceremonies has always been carried out in the pueblos, some of the old ways had been forgotten as the old people died and the young moved away. But when the younger people hear about the old ceremonies, they often decide that they would like to revive them. Daisy often has orders for the double-horned wedding jars, which are used for wedding ceremonies. She also makes small basket-shaped bowls for sacred cornmeal. Cornmeal, long a staple in the diet of Pueblo people, is widely used in religious ceremonies by southwestern tribes. A sprinkling of it, often mixed with powdered turquoise, is used as a blessing. Daisy also makes whistles for the priests like the one she found at Sikyatki.

Daisy's grandchildren are taking up Zuni crafts. Marlin carves stones, and Randy makes silver jewelry. Daisy's granddaughter Cheryl often comes from Gallup to stay with her, and Daisy is teaching pottery making to her. Although Cheryl is only nine, she is learning the skill just as Daisy did at that age. Daisy takes Cheryl's little bowls with her when she demonstrates away from Zuni. In teaching the craft to her grandchild, Daisy is repeating the ancient cycle.

CHAPTER VIII

Recognition In Zuni And Beyond

For the Shalako ceremony of 1973, Daisy and Sidney volunteered to build one of the houses to honor a Shalako. It was a generous act because they had to undertake the expense of building a new house, but it is an honor to own one of the houses blessed by a Shalako. Since there are six houses built each year, there are many Shalako houses in Zuni. For their house, Daisy and Sidney constructed a large cinder block structure across the yard from the old adobe house.

In the fall, certain priests in the Zuni religious societies choose the date for Shalako Day, which will take place some time in late November or early December. Then the women begin their preparation. They grind cornmeal, bake bread, and just before Shalako, make enough mutton stew for the feast. At dusk on the day of the house blessing, a masked Shalako, accompanied by priests and singers, arrives at the house. One of the priests blesses the house with prayer plumes and sacred cornmeal. Then everyone present eats an enormous feast. More people from the pueblo and outside visitors crowd into the house. They all bring their own chairs until not an inch of floor space is left. Finally, after midnight the dancing begins. In spite of the awkward costume the Shalako dances with grace and nimbleness through the long hours. Usually, two men take turns dancing in the costume for it requires great energy. Other dancers come and go, but the Shalako stays with the house he blesses. Daisy's Shalako house is not entirely completed, but she uses the finished portion for her workshop. She would like to add a second story sometime.

Besides Shalako, other honors came to Daisy as a result of her growing reputation. Once again, she has begun to travel. Now the purpose of her trips is not for study, but to teach others how to make fine pottery. In late 1973 her pottery was exhibited at the M. H. de Young Memorial Museum in San Francisco. She and Sidney went to San Francisco; both of them worked during the exhibit. Daisy held special demonstrations and fired her pottery at the museum. They made many friends during their stay. When they left, they sprinkled sacred cornmeal and powdered turquoise over the museum staff that gathered to see them off.

In the spring of 1974 all of the descendants of Nampeyo exhibited their work at the Muckenthaler Cultural Center in Fullerton, California. Daisy, her sister Rachel, and some of Rachel's daughters went to southern California to demonstrate during the exhibit. At about this time, all of the descendants of Nampeyo decided to sign their work using their own names with Nampeyo's name added last so that the pottery can be identified as coming from her family. Daisy's signature then became Daisy Hooee Nampeyo. They also published a list of their designs in the newspaper, claiming that they are the property of the Nampeyo family. In this way, they hope to establish a kind of copyright on the patterns so that other potters will not use their designs.

Daisy at work in her kitchen. Note the stone metate on which she grinds the paint.

Daisy with students at the Honolulu Academy of Arts in 1974. She is showing them how she decorates her pots.

One of the pots that Daisy exhibited in Fullerton is known as the "people pot." The design is a favorite of hers; the whole family uses it extensively. The pattern consists of many parallel, curving lines that harmonize beautifully with the contour of the bowl. Daisy remembers that Nampeyo told her that each of the lines represents a person. In ancient times this was the method of counting the people. The lines curve over the bowl to symbolize the migrations of the people from the time they first appeared in this world. The people pot, then, is a picture of the Hopi migration legends.

As Daisy grows older, she remembers more and more of the stories Nampeyo told her. The stories are repeated less and less often at First Mesa, and because she was so close to her grandmother, Daisy knows more of the old legends than other members of her family. Daisy sees Hopis of the younger generation losing the old beliefs. "But I understand and I believe what my grandmother told me," she often says. Believing the old legends is a firm part of her character, and she feels that it is more important than ever to remember them and record them.

When the people pot was shown at Fullerton, visitors at the gallery asked Daisy how she put the complex design on the pot before she painted it. They could not believe it could be done freehand. Daisy told them the ancient people had no pencils for drawing or measuring the design. Like every design on Hopi pottery, the curving lines of the people pot are painted freehand with a steady, sure sweep of the artist's wrist.

In the fall of 1974, Daisy's travels took her overseas to Hawaii. She spent a week at the Honolulu Academy of Arts showing students of ceramics how to transform a mound of

Daisy and the students in Honolulu have just finished the last step—firing the pots. Just the slightest breeze might crack a pot as it cools.

ROAD

grey clay into a fine pot. Many came each day during the week to see her coil the clay, polish the pots, and finally, the last day, fire the pottery. During the week she attracted more and more interested students.

Daisy loves to share her skills with all who will listen, but she is happy to get back to Zuni. She and Sidney still live in the house that she built. The Shalako house serves as her workshop. When the weather turns brisk in the fall and winter, Daisy works in the kitchen of the adobe house. She sets her dried and polished pots on a spotless worktable in the center of the kitchen. Arranged on the table are a few pieces of pottery, a metate on which dried bee weed paint is ground, and some colorful polishing stones. In another room the whine of Sidney's lapidary wheel breaks the stillness while he works at his craft. The only other sound is the occasional snap of fragrant juniper from the stove. Daisy picks up a slender yucca fiber brush and paints an even line that encircles the neck of the bowl. Known as a lifeline, it is painted as a closed circle when a woman is past her child-bearing years. When she is still having children, a tiny opening is left in the lifeline. Daisy closes hers now that she is in her sixties, just as she remembers Nampeyo did when Daisy sat beside her.

When the women come to her workshop, Daisy puts a shawl over her head and crosses the yard to the workshop. The shawl frames her large expressive eyes. Her hair, which she coils on top of her head, is still a rich, glossy black. Like other Hopi women her age, Daisy is small—only a little over five feet tall—and plump.

Each day about twenty-six women come to learn Daisy's techniques. Daisy willingly gives her time and energy to

Painting the pots takes great skill and a steady hand. Daisy freely shares her skill with people at home and far away.

anyone who is interested in learning how to make pottery in the old way, but anyone who sees Daisy learns something even more meaningful than her techniques. Because she is generous of spirit, she always shares her thoughts as well as her skills with her students. She wants them to have some understanding of the importance of the old ways in a world that is fast changing.

"The Earth Mother gives you everything," she says while her sensitive hands mold the sides of a pot. "The Earth gives you the clay to shape the pot. You don't have to buy it. You shape the clay with your hands, not with a wheel. Bee weed, mustard, and wheat can be boiled to make the paint. You don't buy the paint or the brushes. You chew yucca fibers for them. After I make my pots, I smooth the roughness with sandstone that comes from the mountain. Then you burnish it with a slip, that's just clay. And the burnishing rock comes from the earth." She lifts up a glassy-surfaced stone that fits her cupped palm as though it were set there by a silversmith. "You fire the pottery outside, not with a kiln. You use manure or bones for fuel.

"The ancient people had nothing. But they used these things from the earth and they used their hands, and they made pots to cook in and spoons for eating. They made everything they needed.

"The Earth Mother gives you all these things. And you use them and your hands and you work hard. Then you will have something fine, made in the old, old way."

THE AUTHOR

Carol Fowler is a free-lance writer who has contributed both short stories and nonfiction articles to a number of young people's magazines, including *Ingenue, Twelve-Fifteen,* and *Teen Time.*

Her biography of Daisy Hooee Nampeyo was sparked by work on her first book for children, *Contributions of Women: Art.* Not only was she impressed by the Hopi potter's artistic stature, but she also felt that Ms. Hooee's life would be of special interest to young readers. The resulting book is the first full-length biography of Daisy Hooee Nampeyo.

The photographs are reproduced through the courtesy of Edward Curtis, The North American Indian *(1907-1930); Carol Fowler; Heard Museum; Honolulu Academy of Arts; Museum of New Mexico; Daisy Hooee Nampeyo; Sotheby Parke Bernet, Inc.; Southwest Museum; Tournament of Roses Association; U.S. Department of the Interior*

[redacted]

OTHER BIOGRAPHIES
IN THIS SERIES ARE

William Beltz

Robert Bennett

Crazy Horse

Geronimo

Oscar Howe

Pauline Johnson

Chief Joseph

Maria Martinez

George Morrison

Michael Naranjo

Osceola

Powhatan

Red Cloud

Sacagawea

Sequoyah

Sitting Bull

Maria Tallchief

Jim Thorpe

Tomo-chi-chi

Pablita Velarde

William Warren

Annie Wauneka